IMAGES
*of America*

# LOS ANGELES
# MEMORIAL COLISEUM

10·18

COLLEGE FOOTBALL HALFTIME SHOW, C. 1940S.

*All photos used by permission of the Los Angeles Memorial Coliseum and the Los Angeles Memorial Sports Arena, except where noted.*

# INTRODUCTION

I am sitting in Section 6, Row 44, Seat 1, at the Los Angeles Memorial Coliseum. While I am the only one here, I have seen the stadium packed with 90,000 strong. Yet somehow, empty on this breezy spring day, it is no less dramatic. I was interested in doing this book to document not just the well-known events that occurred here, but also the more obscure events, because it's the combination of both that give one a full appreciation of this site. It is what separates this grand stadium from others. It's what, I believe, allows you to make the case that the Los Angeles Memorial Coliseum is the most historic stadium in America (if not the world.)

No other place has hosted two Olympiads. Two Super Bowls. A World Series. Countless classic college football matchups featuring both USC and UCLA. The Los Angeles Dodgers. The Coliseum hosted six professional football teams (Rams, Dons, Chargers, and Raiders of the NFL, the Express of the USFL, and the Extreme of the short-lived XFL.), as well as the Aztecs Soccer team and dozens of world-class track events. There have been landmark appearances by John F. Kennedy, Dwight Eisenhower, F.D.R., Charles Lindbergh, General Patton, Nelson Mandela, and Pope John Paul II. The entertainment roster has included the Rolling Stones, Bruce Springsteen, Pink Floyd, and The Who. Not to forget other notable crowd pleasers, such as Evel Knievel, the Harlem Globetrotters (in front of the largest United States basketball crowd on record), prizefighter Jack Dempsey, tennis great Don Budge, football star Red Grange, and baseball icons such as Mickey Mantle, Willie Mays, Ted Williams, Hank Aaron, and Stan Musial. And the motocross, skiing, ice skating, rodeos, boat shows, circuses, fireworks shows, Pontifical Masses, auto races, Boy Scout jamborees... it is staggering. And it is significant.

Construction on the Coliseum took less than two years, with ground-breaking ceremonies held on December 21, 1921, and work completed on time and on budget, May 1, 1923 (initial costs were $800,000.) It opened in June 1923, with the first football game being played on October 23, 1923, with the USC hosting Pomona College before a crowd of 12,836. From 1930–31, the Coliseum's seating capacity was expanded from 75,000 seats to 101,573 in preparation for the Opening Ceremonies of the Xth Olympiad on July 30, 1932. Twenty-one-year-old Babe Didrikson won the hurdles and javelin, and took second in the high jump. Her heroics, along with American Eddie Tolan's double in the 100 and 200 meters, were among the Games' highlights.

Over the next two decades, the Coliseum hosted many other significant sports events including the 1936 Olympic Trials, the annual Coliseum relays, etc. But college football games were the most showcased events during this time, featuring both USC and UCLA (USC continues to call the Coliseum home; UCLA played there from 1926–1981).

In 1946, the Los Angeles Rams arrived from Cleveland, ushering in the pro football era. They remained until 1979, and through the years featured such hall-of-famers as Bob Waterfield, Norm Van Brocklin, Merlin Olsen, and Deacon Jones. They won the NFL title in 1951, a divisional championship in 1955, but then remained out of contention until 1967.

In 1958, the baseball Dodgers arrived from Brooklyn. For four seasons, the Coliseum was their home, providing one of the odder stadium configurations. Three banks of lights were added, dugouts and a press box built, and two screens were put into place—one behind home plate, and the other located from the left field foul pole to centerfield. This was because it was only 251 feet from the foul pole to home plate!

Opening day for the Dodgers at the Coliseum was on April 18, 1958, with over 78,000 fans in attendance. In 1959, a football game between USC and Ohio State was played at the Coliseum, and an hour after completion, the first World Series game in California was played (the Dodgers defeated the White Sox in that series, 4–2). The 1959 baseball all-star game at the Coliseum saw the American League defeat the National League, 5–3. And in only four seasons the Dodgers set several attendance records at the Coliseum, including 92,706 for Game Five of the 1959 World Series and 93,103 for a May 7, 1959 exhibition against the Yankees on Roy Campanella Night (this is the still the single largest crowd in Major League history; the largest event in Coliseum history was a speech made by Billy Graham on September 8, 1963. The event attracted 134,254). In 1959, the Los Angeles Memorial Sports Arena joined the Coliseum in the Exposition Park complex. A chapter is included in this book on the arena.

Super Bowl I was held at the Coliseum on January 27, 1967. Vince Lombardi's Green Bay Packers defeated the Kansas City Chiefs, 35–10. The game returned in 1973, with the Miami Dolphins defeating the Washington Redskins, 14–7 in Super Bowl VII.

In 1984, the Coliseum was declared a State and Federal Historical Landmark, the same year the Olympics returned. During this XXIII Olympiad, 23-year-old Carl Lewis duplicated Jesse Owens' 1936 track and field grand slam by winning the 100 and 200 meters and the long jump, and anchoring the 4x100 meter relay.

From 1982–1994, the Los Angeles Raiders played football at the Coliseum. Prior to their 1993 season, the Coliseum underwent a $15 million renovation. The floor was lowered 11 feet and the running track was removed to create a more intimate stadium. Fourteen new rows of seats were added down low, bringing fans closer to the playing field. During this renovation, the locker rooms and public restrooms were also upgraded.

Southern California's damaging January 1994 earthquake hit the Coliseum hard, requiring some $93 million of repairs. And, in 1995, a new $6 million press box was constructed. Today, the USC Trojans are the lone, steady tenant at the Coliseum. The word is still out on whether another professional sports team will ever move in again.

It's getting late now, so I guess it's time to go. I think I'll walk down on that famous field, up those stairs, and out through the Peristyle arches. Where I'll get goosebumps. Like I always do when I leave this illustrious place.

# One

# BUILDING
# THE COLISEUM

THE BUILDING IS UNDERWAY, DECEMBER 1921. This stunning aerial view, shot by blimp, dramatically depicts the Coliseum as it takes shape around an abandoned gravel pit. At the time, the population of Los Angeles was just 576,673, yet this was to be a 76,000 seat stadium. Clearly, the planning group foresaw the growth that was to come.

**DECEMBER 1921.** Still barely more than a gravel pit, this shot was taken from on top of where the main tunnel would eventually be. You can see the famous Peristyle arches starting to take shape at the upper right.

PERISTYLE CONSTRUCTION, 1921.

**DECEMBER 1921.** This shot looks west from the site of where the Peristyle will be. The dirt being dug up from the gravel pit was actually used to help shape the walls of the Coliseum. The emerging tunnel can be seen at upper left.

December 1921, Looking Toward Tunnel.

**Looking Toward the North Side, 1923.** With the Peristyle all but complete, the rest of the structure continues to take shape.

**Winter 1922.** It was originally called the Los Angeles Memorial Colosseum, as a tribute to those who gave their lives in World War I (the spelling was modeled after the Roman Colosseum). But by July 1920, the spelling had changed to "Coliseum".

**THE JOB IS DONE, 1923.** This is one of the first completed views of the Coliseum, before the stage was constructed for opening ceremonies.

**NEARING COMPLETION, 1923.** Much of the dirt that has been excavated remains at what will soon be mid-field.

**OUTSIDE LOOKING IN, 1923.** Architect John Parkinson's masterpiece is complete, and just weeks away from the festive opening.

**THE MEN WHO BUILT THE COLISEUM, 1923.** Many of the workers, who completed this building both on time and on budget, pose on the just erected seats.

**A VIEW OF THE ARCHES, 1921.** With no workers present, the abandoned site almost resembles an archeological discovery site.

COLISEUM CONSTRUCTION, 1922. The south (right) stands are almost completed.

WORK ON THE UPPER LEVEL HAS BEGUN, 1922.

**PERISTYLE CONSTRUCTION, 1921.** The famous Peristyle arches begin to take shape.

**WORKERS LAYING IN THE SEATS, 1922.**

THE TOP SECTION NEARS COMPLETION, 1923.

THE MAIN ENTRANCE TUNNEL FOR ATHLETES TAKES SHAPE, 1922.

BUILDING THE COLISEUM, 1922. It looks ancient, but the banner promotes what is to become the newest, most spectacular sports building in the country.

AERIAL SHOT OF THE COMPLETED COLISEUM, 1923.

**THE COLISEUM SET FOR FOOTBALL, SEPTEMBER 25, 1930.** Construction is underway to add seats to the upper level in preparation for the 1932 Olympic Summer Games.

**WORKING ON THE RENOVATIONS, JUNE 5, 1930.** Workers atop the Coliseum pour concrete as work progresses on the addition of 30,00 new seats.

JUNE 19TH, 1930. Renovations are underway to add on the 30,000 extra seats that will be needed to hold Olympic spectators in 1932.

NOVEMBER 11, 1930. Renovation continues along the top level.

22

THE COLISEUM SET FOR FOOTBALL, NOVEMBER 13, 1930. The construction to add additional seats to accommodate the approaching 1932 Olympics can be seen at the stadium's farthest reaches.

THE OLYMPIC PLAQUES AND COLISEUM OFFICE ENTRANCEWAY, C. 1950.

**Exterior of the Coliseum, c. 1950s.** The neon Olympic rings were installed on the Peristyle in 1953.

**Artist's Rendering of the Exposition Park Area, c. 1960s.**

**COMMEMORATIVE STONE AT COLISEUM ENTRANCE.** An actual stone from the original Olympic Stadium in Greece (the Altis Olympia) is on display at the Peristyle. A similar-sized stone from the Colosseum in Rome flanks the other side of the entrance.

**POSTCARD IMAGE OF THE COLISEUM, 1932.** The back of the card touts the Coliseum as the scene of the upcoming 1932 Olympic Games, the first time the event was ever held in the U.S.

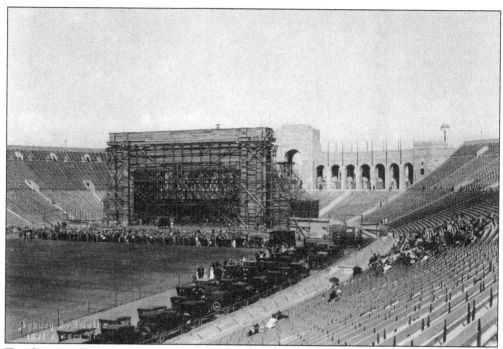

THE STAGE IS BEING BUILT FOR OPENING DAY CEREMONIES, JUNE 1923.

THE STAGE IS SET FOR OPENING DAY CEREMONIES, JUNE 1923. The concert stage for what would be the official opening of the Los Angeles Memorial Coliseum. It sits exactly where stages for the Rolling Stones, U2, Bruce Springsteen, The Who, and others have been built over the last 80 or so years.

**LET THE (FOOTBALL) GAMES BEGIN, OCTOBER 10, 1923.** The very first football game ever to be played at the Coliseum was when the USC Trojans hosted (and defeated, 23–7) Pomona College, before a crowd of just 12,836. A modest beginning for a venue that would later play a huge role in both college and pro football.

**NEW PRESS BOX, 1948.** Costing just over $173,000, the view from this perch still provides one of the greater views in all of sports, college, pro, or otherwise.

PRESS ENTRANCE, 1947.

AERIAL VIEW, C. 1960s. The Coliseum, the Sports Arena, and the Olympic Swimming Stadium dominate Exposition Park. Just to the right of the Coliseum is the Los Angeles Museum of Natural History.

AERIAL VIEW, C. 1960s. The Harbor Freeway (110) can now be seen, running north into downtown Los Angeles.

**AERIAL SHOT OF THE COLISEUM, C. 1940S.** The area known during the holidays as "Christmas Tree Lane" can be seen just above the Peristyle. The 110 freeway has yet to be built just above that.

**DAMAGE FROM THE JANUARY 1994 NORTHRIDGE EARTHQUAKE.** The devastating quake caused much damage to the Coliseum, including buckled concrete and cracked entrance ways, as seen here. (Photo by Raul Robles.)

**EARTHQUAKE DAMAGE TO THE PERISTYLE, JANUARY 1994.** The Coliseum's trademark archway took a major hit from the quake, and has since been repaired and reinforced. (Photo by Raul Robles.)

**THE COLISEUM FLOOR BEING LOWERED, 1993.** Prior to the 1993 football season, the Coliseum underwent a $15 million renovation. The Coliseum's floor was lowered 11 feet and the running track was removed to create a more intimate stadium. (Photos by Raul Robles.)

ADDITIONAL SHOTS OF THE COLISEUM FLOOR BEING LOWERED, 1993. Fourteen new rows of seats (approximately 8,000 seats) were added down low, bringing fans closer to the playing field (the first rows of seats between the goalposts are a maximum of 54 feet from the sideline, instead of the previous 120 feet). During this renovation, the locker rooms and public restrooms were also upgraded. (Photos by Raul Robles.)

The Coliseum Electronic
Scoreboard Being Installed,
February 18, 1972.

**OLYMPIC SWIMMING STADIUM RENOVATION, 2002.** This shot looks into the pool area from the top row of the Coliseum. (Photo taken by author.)

**TIME CAPSULE MARKER.** In the Peristyle courtyard, a copy of Bud Greenspan's *16 Days of Glory*, the official film of the 1984 Summer Olympic Games, is buried. The capsule will be opened in July 2084. (Photo taken by author.)

**ATHLETIC BUILDING ENTRANCE, MAY 7, 1951.** Pictured is William Nicholas (left), general manager of the Coliseum, greeting Paul H. Helms, founder and sponsor of the Helms Athletic Foundation. They are dedicating the new Coliseum Athletic Building. The man on the right is Alan Ewen. (Photo courtesy of Amateur Athletic Foundation.)

**ATHLETIC BUILDING ENTRANCE, TODAY.** Located under the tunnel, this is the entrance to the locker rooms, coaches quarters, and team meeting rooms. (Photo taken by author.)

**EMERGING FROM THE TUNNEL, TODAY.** Standing here, at the entrance to the field, it is incredible to think about all those who have graced this site during the Olympics, the countless football games, the World Series, and even Warren Beatty and Julie Christie, during that wonderful closing scene in 1978's *Heaven Can Wait*. (Photo taken by author.)

**COLISEUM HISTORIC MARKERS NEAR MAIN OFFICE ENTRANCE.** The top plaque is the National Historic marker, the bottom is the State Historical Marker (No. 960). (Photo taken by author.)

**HISTORIC PALM TREE IN EXPOSITION PARK.** At one boundary of Exposition Park, looking west toward the Coliseum Peristyle, a famous tree sits. As the plaque explains, it stood for more than 25 years at the entrance of the Southern Pacific Railway Station, a landmark to thousands of citizens who visited and lived in Los Angeles. In 1914, the small piece of history was replanted here, right near a larger piece of history, visible in the background. (Photo taken by author.)

# Two

# General Sports
# at the Coliseum

Opening Ceremonies, 1932 Olympic Games, July 30, 1932. (Photo courtesy of Amateur Athletic Foundation.)

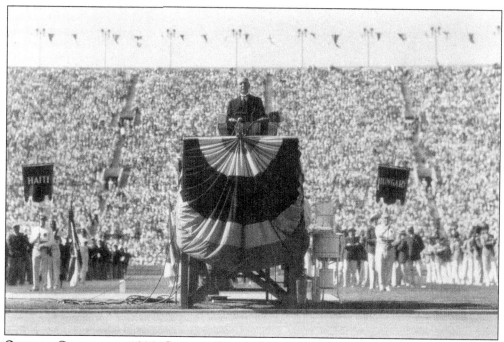

OPENING CEREMONIES, 1932 OLYMPIC GAMES, JULY 30, 1932. Dr. Robert Gordon Sproul, president, University of California, during the Games' dedication address. (Photo courtesy of Amateur Athletic Foundation.)

OPENING CEREMONIES, 1932 OLYMPIC GAMES, JULY 30, 1932. United States Vice President Charles Curtis opens the games at the Coliseum. (Photo courtesy of Amateur Athletic Foundation.)

**OPENING CEREMONIES, 1932 OLYMPIC GAMES, JULY 30, 1932.** Despite the Depression the nation was involved in, 105,000 turned out for the Xth Olympiad Opening Ceremonies. (Photo courtesy of Amateur Athletic Foundation.)

OPENING CEREMONIES, 1932
OLYMPIC GAMES, JULY 30, 1932.
The U.S. is passing the Tribune of
Honor. (Photo courtesy of Amateur
Athletic Foundation.)

PREPARATION FOR OPENING
CEREMONIES, 1932 OLYMPIC
GAMES. (Photo courtesy of Amateur
Athletic Foundation.)

**AWARD PRESENTATION, 1932 OLYMPICS.** Pictured, left to right, are Americans Edward Jennings, Charles Kieffer, and Joseph Schauers, receiving their Gold Medals for Rowing. (Photo courtesy of Amateur Athletic Foundation.)

**RAFER JOHNSON.** Rafer Johnson lights the torch at the Opening Ceremonies of the 1984 Olympic Summer Games. This officially made the Coliseum the only stadium on earth to host two Olympiads.

**BARRY O'BRIEN.** O'Brien is shown competing during the Los Angeles Coliseum Relays, c. early 1950s. The relays were a popular annual track and field meet and O'Brien was its most honored athlete. He competed in nine of them (1950–59), was the shot put champ at the relays seven times, and won medals in the '52, '56 and '60 Olympic Games.

**JUAN ZABALA, 1932.** Zabala, representing Argentina, was the 1932 Olympic Marathon Champion at the Coliseum.

OLYMPICS EQUESTRIAN EVENT, 1932 SUMMER GAMES.

SPRINTERS RALPH METCALFE AND ED TOLAN, 1932 OLYMPICS. Metcalfe won silver and bronze medals at the '32 Olympic Games. Eddie Tolan, his U.S. teammate, won the gold in both events. In the 100, Tolan and Metcalfe finished in a dead heat and judges took several hours to declare a winner. In the 200, it was discovered after the race that Metcalfe had started three or four feet behind the other runners. Offered a re-run by Olympic officials, he declined rather than jeopardize his country's sweep in the event.

**SKI JUMP EXHIBITION, FEBRUARY 27, 1938.** This was the First Annual Southern California Open Ski Meet. Sponsored by the Lake Arrowhead Ski Club, it was the first ski jump tournament in southern California to be held on man-made snow. The archways in the Peristyle are sealed off, probably to cut down any wind that might have upset the jumper's balance in this, one of the most unlikely events ever staged at the Coliseum.

**Ski Jump Exhibition, February 27, 1938, at Night.** Twenty thousand people attended this event. Just below the center of the picture, huge blocks of ice are visible. When more "snow" was needed, they were shaved and quickly hauled up to the makeshift slope.

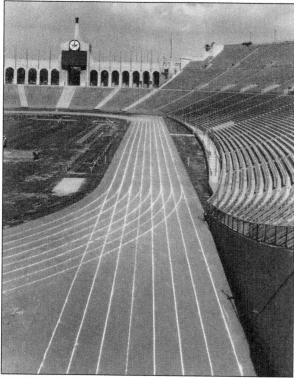

**BOXING AT THE COLISEUM, SEPTEMBER 15, 1972.** The ring, set up in the west part of the Coliseum near the tunnel, was set up for the fight between Mando Ramos and Chango Carmona. Note the Channel 5 KTLA broadcast truck.

**AFTER THE 1932 OLYMPIC GAMES.**

SETTING UP FOR TRACK AND FIELD IN THE 1932 OLYMPIC GAMES.

USC TRACK MEET, C. 1940S.

PREPARING FOR A TRACK MEET, APRIL 4, 1925. On April 25, 1995, the Pavo Nurmi International Meet at the Coliseum was held, in honor of the legendary Finnish long distance runner, nicknamed "The Flying Finn."

THE ORIGINAL PRESS BOX, APRIL 25, 1925. Located at field level, these people are getting ready for the Pavo Nurmi International Meet at the Coliseum.

COLISEUM RELAYS, MAY 21, 1948. Just after World War II, the "World's Fastest Human" was Melvin "Mel" Patton. "Pell Mell," as he was nicknamed in the late 1940s, made his mark in track and field while a student at the University of Southern California, where Hall of Famer Dean Cromwell coached him. In this photo, he is fourth from the right.

HIGH-JUMPING DURING THE COLISEUM RELAYS, C. 1940S.

THE PAVO NURMI INTERNATIONAL MEET AT THE COLISEUM, APRIL 25, 1925.

COLISEUM BILLBOARD, 1959. Upcoming competitors pose against a billboard advertising the popular Coliseum relays. (Photo courtesy of Amateur Athletic Foundation.)

BOXING SET UP AT THE COLISEUM, C. 1970S.

OLGA CONNOLLY. Connolly is pictured throwing the discus at the Coliseum Relays, May 5, 1957. In 1956, she won a gold medal at the Melbourne Olympics for Czechoslovakia while competing under her maiden name Olga Fikotova. At that Olympics, she met America's gold medal winning hammer thrower, Hal Connolly. They later married, and Olga began to compete for the U.S.

Motorcycle Racing at the Coliseum, c. 1945.

Soccer at the Coliseum, c. 1966.

Off Road Racing at the Coliseum, c. late-1970s. These cars are heading up a specially built ramp to actually speed through the Peristyle arches.

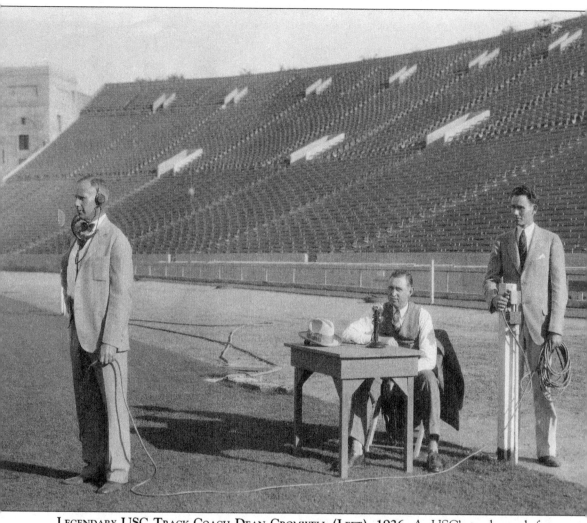

**LEGENDARY USC TRACK COACH DEAN CROMWELL (LEFT), 1926.** As USC's track coach for 38 years, he produced Olympic champions in every Olympiad held from 1912 until his retirement in 1948. He served as an Olympic track coach in 1928 and as head Olympic coach in 1948.

## Three

# SPECIAL EVENTS AT THE COLISEUM

**DWIGHT EISENHOWER AT THE COLISEUM, AUGUST 5, 1952.** Before addressing the VFW Convention, Eisenhower is seen here with Governor Goodwin Knight (on the left).

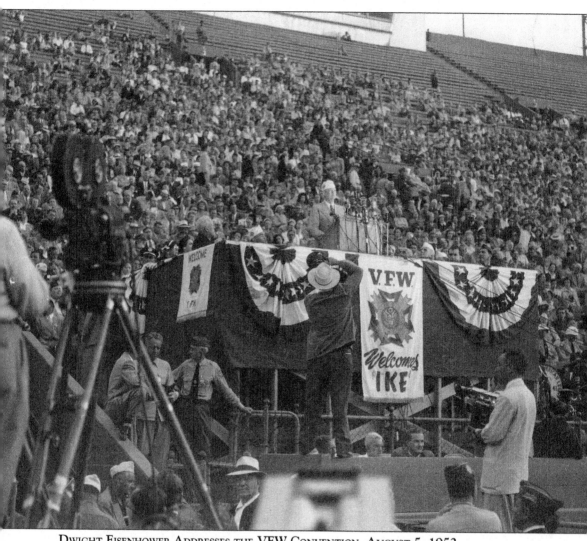

Dwight Eisenhower Addresses the VFW Convention, August 5, 1952.

RELIGIOUS SERVICE, C. 1940S.

COLISEUM CIRCUS, C. 1920S.

**SHRINE CONVENTION AND ELECTRICAL PAGEANT, JULY 11, 1929.** A model steamboat is rolled across the Coliseum at this event that 60,000 people attended. Shrine pageants at the Coliseum featured massive, colorful floats and parades of true grandeur.

**BOAT SHOW, C. 1940S.**

CHRISTMAS TREE LANE, C. 1940s. Starting in 1936, during the holidays, 32 trees were lit with Christmas lights along this park leading up to the Coliseum. Annually, an average of 100,000 autos would make their way along the route.

CHRISTMAS TREE LANE AT NIGHT, C. 1940s.

THE 1953 Scout-a-Rama.

ANOTHER VIEW OF THE 1953 Scout-a-Rama.

**REVEREND BILLY GRAHAM.** The Reverend's landmark appearance on September 8, 1963, brought in an attendance of 134,354 people, the largest single event in Coliseum history.

**THE DAY OF BILLY GRAHAM'S RECORD-SETTING APPEARANCE, SEPTEMBER 8, 1963.** Graham (pictured on the far right) is seen here with Coliseum general manager William H. Nicholas (far left) and County Board Supervisor Kenneth Hahn (third from the left).

ANOTHER VIEW OF BILLY GRAHAM'S APPEARANCE, SEPTEMBER 8, 1963.

**JOHN ANSON FORD AND ESTHER WILLIAMS, 1952.** Supervisor John Anson Ford and swimming star Esther Williams help commemorate the unveiling of the plaques commemorating the 1932 Olympics with a ceremonial Olympic torch.

A SCHOOL EVENT IDENTIFIED AS "FIELD DAY," C. 1940S.

**THE SHRINER'S TAKE OVER THE COLISEUM, 1950.** From June 19–23, 1950, the 76th Imperial Council Session moved into the Coliseum, dressing it up with elaborate props and costuming.

**THE LIGHTING OF THE CHRISTMAS TREES CEREMONY, C. 1950s.** A festive holiday choir rings in the season under the Peristyle.

**THE LIGHTING OF THE CHRISTMAS TREES CEREMONY, c. 1950s.** A festive holiday choir rings in the season under the Peristyle.

**LIGHTING THE CHRISTMAS TREES, c. 1950s.** From left, Supervisor Leonard J. Roach, his wife Eleanor, and Coliseum manager William H. Nicholas prepare to pull the switch in the annual Coliseum tree lighting ceremony.

**THE MARY'S HOUR DEVOTIONAL SERVICE, MAY 6, 1951.** This large Catholic Mass attracted 60,000 faithful. Years later, this service was moved to Dodger Stadium by team owner Walter O'Malley.

**THE KENNEDY PLAQUE.** This marks the spot from where John F. Kennedy addressed the Democratic faithful on June 15, 1960, accepting the party nomination for president.

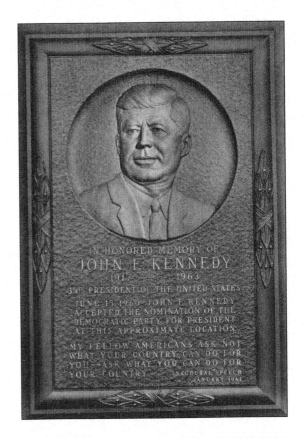

**SHERIFF'S RODEO, AUGUST 22, 1948.** Sheriff Eugene Biscailuz rides the bronc during the popular Sheriff's Rodeo, which attracted 100,854 on this day, and is evidenced by the packed stands.

**MICK JAGGER.** On October 11, 1981, the Rolling Stones drew 98,876 fans.

THE ROLLING STONES STAGE SET AT THE COLISEUM, OCTOBER 11, 1981.

PAPAL MASS, SEPTEMBER 15, 1987. Over 100,000 people were on hand to witness Pope John Paul II. The scoreboard reads "Papal Liturgy" and downtown Los Angeles is visible off to the right.

**COLISEUM FIREWORKS SHOW, C. 1950S.** Many Los Angelenos fondly remember flocking to the Coliseum for the annual 4th of July spectacular, such as this one.

# Four

# FOOTBALL
# AT THE COLISEUM

**LOS ANGELES DONS HOLIDAY PROMOTION, C. 1948.** From 1946 until 1949, the Dons (of the All-America Football Conference) played at the Coliseum. This float was part of a small parade they staged in December 1949. (Photo courtesy of Amateur Athletic Foundation.)

COLISEUM BACKDROP, C. EARLY 1950S. Former pro football player Glen Dobbs (left) and local writer Rube Samuelsen tape a TV show at KTLA, Hollywood. The backdrop is a scrim featuring a Coliseum blowup. (Photo courtesy of Amateur Athletic Foundation.)

THE USC MARCHING BAND, C. 1950S.

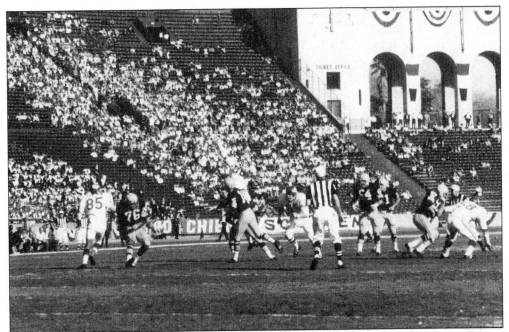

**Super Bowl I, January 15, 1967.** Vince Lombardi's Green Bay Packers defeated the Kansas City Chiefs, 35–10 in the very first Super Bowl. Note the number of empty seats.

**Presentation of the Very First Super Bowl Trophy, January 15, 1967.** Legendary Packer coach Vince Lombardi receives the award from Pete Rozelle.

USC Football Game, c. 1940s.

USC Football Game, c. 1930s.

The USC Marching Band, c. 1950s.

USC Football Game Halftime Show, c. 1950s.

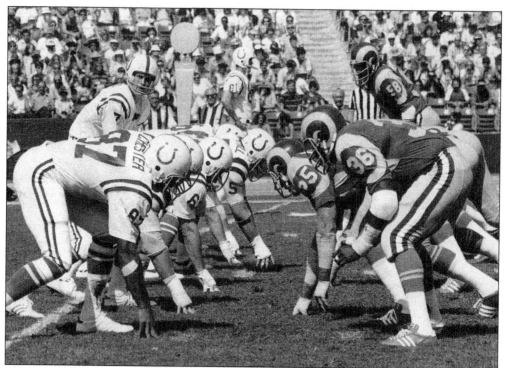

**PRO FOOTBALL GAME, 1970s.** Colt quarterback Bert Jones is seen here leading his team against the Rams.

**PRO FOOTBALL AERIAL SHOT, C. 1970s.** The ever-present Goodyear Blimp hovers above a Los Angeles Rams game. Note the tight parking all around.

**RAMS GAME, c. 1960s.** Note the old-style, cumbersome network TV camera.

**RAMS GAME AT NIGHT, 1960s.** Ram teams of the '60s featured such greats as Deacon Jones, Merlin Olsen, and Jack Pardee.

USC FOOTBALL GAME, C. 1940S.

USC FOOTBALL, C. 1940S. This shot was taken from a second story room in the Peristyle.

STARS OF THE LOS ANGELES RAMS, 1946. Pictured are, from left, Washington, Waterfield, Holovak, and Harmon, the first year the Rams came to the Coliseum. (Photo courtesy of Amateur Athletic Foundation.)

THE COLISEUM LIT BY A MOBILE LIGHTING RIG, C. 1954.

**SUPER BOWL VII, JANUARY 14, 1973.** Led by quarterback Bob Griese and Coach Don Shula, the Miami Dolphins (who were undefeated that season) downed the Washington Redskins, 14–7.

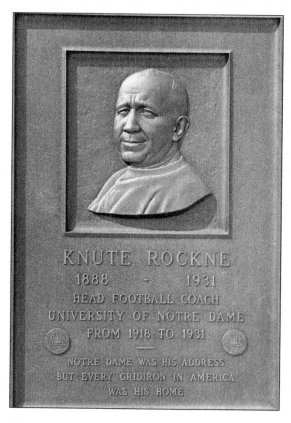

KNUTE ROCKNE
1888 - 1931
HEAD FOOTBALL COACH
UNIVERSITY OF NOTRE DAME
FROM 1918 TO 1931

NOTRE DAME WAS HIS ADDRESS
BUT EVERY GRIDIRON IN AMERICA
WAS HIS HOME

**KNUTE ROCKNE PLAQUE IN THE PERISTYLE'S MEMORIAL COURT OF HONOR.** This is one of the more than 50 plaques mounted against the sides of the Peristyle, honoring famous coaches, teams, events, etc. The very first plaque, honoring William May Garland, was placed May 20, 1949. Mr. Garland played a big part in the building and promotion of the Coliseum.

**FOOTBALL AT NIGHT, C. 1930s.**
Note the light-colored ball that
was used for evening games.

RAMS GAME, C. 1940s.

**USC Football from the Sky,
c. 1940s.** A packed house watches
the Trojans. The Olympic Swimming
Stadium is visible to the lower left, and
the Los Angeles Museum of Natural
History is just above the Coliseum.

**Joe Namath at the Coliseum,
1977.** Namath played one season at
the Coliseum (1977–1978) with the
Los Angeles Rams before his retirement
from football in 1978. He was elected to
the Pro Football Hall of Fame in 1985.

*Five*

# BASEBALL
# AT THE COLISEUM

**OPENING DAY FOR THE DODGERS, FROM THE SKY, APRIL 18, 1958.** Clearly, baseball was not intended as the primary sport at the Coliseum. Three banks of lights were added for the Dodgers, dugouts were built, a press box was constructed, and two screens were put into place. Note the huge foul territory near third base, and the lack of it behind first.

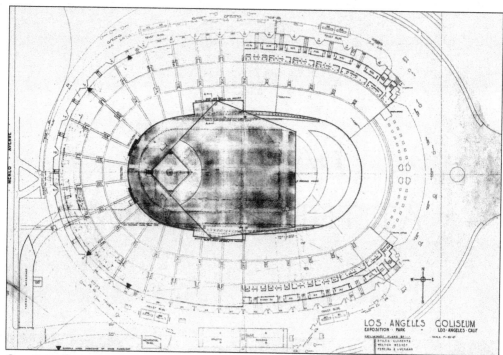

**ORIGINAL COLISEUM BASEBALL BLUEPRINTS, C. 1920s.** USC was actually the first team to play baseball at the Coliseum, and this was their configuration. It differs slightly from the one the Dodgers used.

**MAYOR MORRIS POULSEN AND WALTER O'MALLEY, 1958.** The Los Angeles mayor greets the Dodgers owner at a downtown celebration welcoming the team from Brooklyn.

**Opening Day for the Los Angeles Dodgers at the Coliseum, April 18, 1958.** Comedian Joe E. Brown (center) introduces Dodger skipper Walter Alston (right) to the crowd. Giants manager Bill Rigney looks on (the Giants had also just moved to the west coast from New York). The Dodgers won, 6–5, before a crowd of 78,672.

**The Dodgers Win the Pennant, September 29, 1959.** The Dodgers have just beaten the Milwaukee Braves in the National League Championship Playoff, 6–5 in 12 innings. (They'd next go on to beat the White Sox in the World Series.)

GIL HODGES CROSSES HOMEPLATE AT THE COLISEUM, 1958.

BASEBALL AT THE COLISEUM, 1959. This gives you an idea of the broad expanse that was baseball at the Coliseum.

**A HOT DOG VENDOR AT THE COLISEUM, 1958.** The heights one has to climb to reach the top rows of the Coliseum makes you appreciate the work this guy is doing on a hot summer day.

**THE INFAMOUS LEFT FIELD FENCE, 1958.** Due to the unusually short distance to left field (just 250 feet), a 42-foot screen was erected in an attempt to reduce the number of pop fly home runs. Left-handed Dodger outfielder Wally Moon started hitting pop flies to the opposite field—easy home runs in the Coliseum. These became known as "Moon Shots."

**THE VIEW FROM UP TOP, 1959.** Southern California took to the Dodgers right away, and many games were packed like this, despite the insane distances one could sit from the action.

**RECORD-SETTING WORLD SERIES ATTENDANCE, 1959.** It's top of the sixth, game four of the 1959 World Series between the Dodgers and the Chicago White Sox. As the scoreboard indicates, the attendance is 92,550, a new World Series record (those seats under the scoreboard were about 700 feet from home plate).

**DODGER CHAMPIONSHIP PLAQUE.** One of the more than 50 plaques in the Peristyle's Memorial Court of Honor is one commemorating the 1959 World Champion Los Angeles Dodgers. (Photo taken by author.)

**DODGERS BATTING PRACTICE, 1958.** This view from right-center gives one an idea of what it looked like to play the Coliseum outfield. How different it must have felt from cozy Ebbets Field in Brooklyn.

A Packed Dodger Game, 1958.

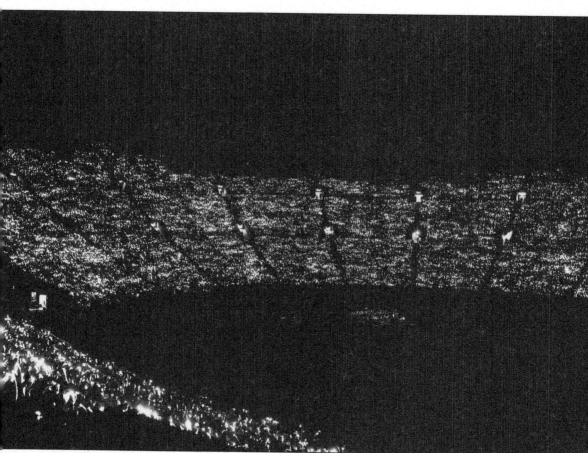

**ROY CAMPANELLA NIGHT, MAY 7, 1959.** Four months before the Dodgers opened in Los Angeles, beloved catcher Roy Campanella was paralyzed in a car accident. A year later, the Dodgers and Yankees (in an exhibition game) drew 93,103 people to the Los Angeles Coliseum to honor Campanella, which still ranks as the largest crowd ever for a major-league game. In a pre-game ceremony, he was wheeled out to second base by his long-time teammate, shortstop Pee Wee Reese. The lights in the Coliseum were turned off, and the fans lit matches to honor him.

*Six*

# The Los Angeles Memorial Sports Arena

**Artist's Rendering of the Los Angeles Memorial Sports Arena, 1959.** The Coliseum is depicted to the upper right of this rendering, which was pictured on the Opening Day program and ticket in 1959.

**BUILDING THE SPORTS ARENA, SEPTEMBER 16, 1958.** Opening ceremonies were less than a year away for the Coliseum's neighbor—a then state-of-the-art arena that would soon be home to both the Los Angeles Lakers basketball team and the Los Angeles Kings hockey team.

**THE SPORTS ARENA NEARS COMPLETION, EARLY 1959.** The "flying-saucer" shape gave the arena a futuristic feel that was popular in the late '50s and early '60s.

UPPER LEVEL CONSTRUCTION, 1958.

RICHARD M. NIXON CHRISTENS THE LOS ANGELES MEMORIAL SPORTS ARENA, JULY 4, 1959.
Then Vice President Nixon dedicates the area in "Recognition of all who served their country
in all wars."

97

**Sports Expo, Opening Day, July 4, 1959.** To demonstrate the all-purpose nature of the arena, on opening day a host of sports exhibitions were conducted, including golf, gymnastics and hockey.

**SPORTS ARENA OPENING DAY CEREMONIES, JULY 4, 1959.** Here, Nixon can be seen near the lower-center of the photo, preparing to address the capacity crowd.

**GOLF EXHIBITIONS, OPENING DAY, JULY 4, 1959.** I cannot imagine how far these people were allowed to hit those balls, considering the place was packed. The woman directly in front of Nixon appears to be lining up a direct hit on the vice president.

**LAKER BASKETBALL AT THE SPORTS ARENA, EARLY 1960s.** When the Lakers moved out from Minneapolis in 1960, this is where they played through 1968, until the Forum opened. Here, Elgin Baylor's Lakers lead the Philadelphia Warriors, 25–17 in the first period.

RICHARD WASHINGTON AT THE SPORTS ARENA, C. MID-1970S. Washington, a forward/center, starred on UCLA's basketball team through in the mid-70s. He is seen here during a game against USC.

**LAKER BASKETBALL, 1965.** Philadelphia 76er Wilt Chamberlain watches the scramble below the hoop.

**THE LOS ANGELES SHARKS, 1972.** Members of the World Hockey Association, the Sharks played at the Sports Arena from 1972–1974. The Kings played here as well in 1967 before moving over to the Forum with the Lakers.

THE SPORTS ARENA, C. 1960. Back when it was an exciting new venue, the Sports Arena packed them in. The Coliseum is located directly behind the arena and the Olympic Swimming Stadium is to the left.

**JETHRO TULL STAGE, C. 1980.** The Viking Ship stage was one of many big rock-and-roll productions to visit the Sports Arena over the years. The Rolling Stones played here back in 1965, and since then it has hosted Bruce Springsteen, U2 (part of their film *Rattle and Hum* was shot here), David Bowie, Billy Joel, Michael Jackson, and many others.

Monster Trucks At The Sports Arena, c. 1990s.

DANNY MANNING, LOS ANGELES CLIPPERS. The Sports Arena was home to the Los Angeles Clippers from 1984 (when the Clippers moved up from San Diego) through the end of the 1999 season (when the team moved to STAPLES Center). The injury-prone Manning was the number one pick of the 1988 draft, and was a member of the Clippers until 1993.

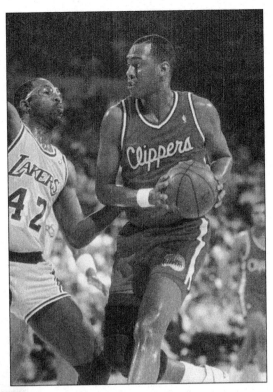

CHARLES SMITH, LOS ANGELES CLIPPERS. Smith, another player from the 1988 draft, was an Olympic teammate of Manning's in the 1988 Games in Seoul, Korea.

LYNN SHACKELFORD DEFENDS AGAINST THE UNIVERSITY OF HOUSTON'S ELVIN HAYS, MARCH 22, 1968.

**DAVID GILMOUR OF PINK FLOYD, 1987.** Pink Floyd played the Sports Arena several times, including *The Wall* tour, which played just two American venues (the Sports Arena and New York's Nassau Coliseum). This photo was taken during the *A Momentary Lapse of Reason* tour.

LOS ANGELES MEMORIAL SPORTS ARENA POSTCARD, C. 1960.

SEAT 8
ROW 9
ENTRY 21A

TICKET FROM THE SPORTS ARENA OPENING CEREMONIES, JULY 4, 1959.

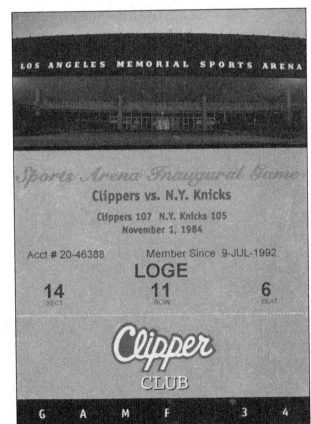

TICKET FROM THE LAST LOS ANGELES CLIPPERS HOME GAME, MAY 5, 1999. I attended this game, and the Clippers lost to the Seattle Supersonics, 107–105. Ironically, the very first game the Clippers ever played here, they defeated the New York Knicks by the same score.

Two Views Of The Exterior Of The Sports Arena, Today. (Photos taken by author)

## Seven

# THE COLISEUM, THEN AND NOW

LOOKING EAST IN HE COLISEUM, 1923 AND TODAY. The stage is set for the opening ceremonies of the Los Angeles Memorial Coliseum, May 1923. Today, the temporary stands sit where the stage was. (Recent photo taken by author.)

**LOOKING WEST FROM UNDER THE PERISTYLE, 1930 AND TODAY.** You can see the construction underway to add seats on top for the Olympics, which was two years away. Also note how the tunnel entrance has changed over the years. Thank you to my son, Charlie, for standing in as the "Now" reference. (Recent photo taken by author.)

GATE TWO, 1921 AND TODAY. The older photo gives you an idea of how the dirt from this one-time gravel pit was used in the shaping and molding of the Coliseum. (Recent photo taken by author.)

**LOOKING TOWARD THE PERISTYLE, 1923 AND TODAY.** The top photo, taken just months before the Coliseum officially opened, is a good representative shot of the wooden bleacher seats that were originally all the Coliseum had. Today you can seat the more conventional "stadium" seats, with my son standing near where the inspector is in the 1923 shot. (Recent photo taken by author.)

**LOOKING TOWARD GATE SIX, 1923 AND TODAY.** The Press Box elevator and tower seen in the "Now" photo were originally built in 1947. Note the heavy landscaping that has also been done since the "Then" photo, taken just before the Coliseum first opened. (Recent photo taken by author.)

**THE PERISTYLE ARCHES, 1923 AND TODAY.** The building has just been finished and three men seem to be inspecting the base of the main arch entryway. Before all of the plaques, the scoreboards, clocks, etc., the archway's almost ancient, elegant, stunningly classic design can be entirely appreciated. (Recent photo taken by author.)

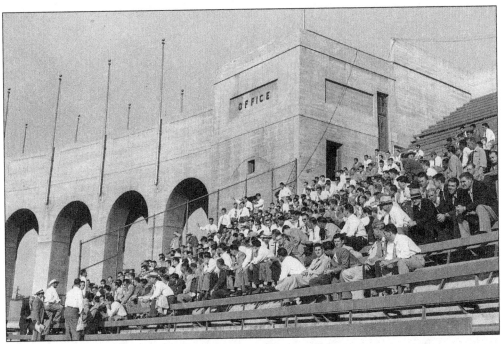

COLISEUM EMPLOYEES GATHERED NEAR THE PERISTYLE, C. 1940 AND SAME AREA TODAY. Back then, 350 ushers were needed for a big event at the Coliseum. Most of them were "regulars"—high school or college students picking up some extra spending money. On the day I shot the recent photo, we had the good fortune to meet the Hitch family, visiting from Green Bay, Wisconsin. For Bill Hitch, the dad, visiting the Coliseum was nothing short of a trip to Mecca. For that, his family is featured here along with Margaret Farnum and my son, Charlie. (Recent photo taken by author.)

**LOOKING IN TOWARD THE TUNNEL AREA, 1922 AND TODAY.** Seat moorings are already embedded in several parts of the stadium, and the area's transformation from gravel pit into world-class stadium is well underway. In the recent shot you can see the press box at the top of the stadium. (Recent photo taken by author.)

LOOKING TOWARD THE PLAYER'S TUNNEL, 1923 AND TODAY. The original bleacher-style benches are in the process of being installed in the older photo. In the recent photo, you can make out the lighter outline of the lower bowl seats that were installed during the 1993 renovation. (Recent photo taken by author.)

**PERISTYLE ARCHES, C. 1920S AND TODAY.** In the older photo, the men are standing near the original, man-operated USC scoreboard. The pedestal to the right of the main archway is where John. F. Kennedy accepted the Democratic nomination for president on July 15, 1960. Ironically, Robert Kennedy's rally in June 1968 was cancelled when he was shot at the Ambassador Hotel on his way to the Coliseum to accept the California Democratic nomination for president. (Recent photo taken by author.)

LOOKING TOWARD THE PERISTYLE FROM THE NORTH SIDE OF THE COLISEUM, 1923 AND TODAY.
(Recent photo taken by author.)

**EXTERIOR OF THE OLYMPIC SWIMMING STADIUM, 2001 AND TODAY.** The stadium next dorr to the Coliseum is currently undergoing a massive overhaul, with plans to open next year. (Photos taken by author.)

**CLOSER: EXTERIOR OF THE OLYMPIC SWIMMING STADIUM, 2001 AND TODAY.** It's being called E.P.I.C.C. (Exposition Park Inter-generational Community Center), and once complete will also house basketball and volleyball facilities. Slated to open in 2003, this center is designed to become a vital part of the community. (Photos taken by author.)

**LOOKING UP THE MAIN STAIRS, 1950 AND TODAY.** Paul Helms (right) co-founded the Helms Sports of Fame Hall in 1936. A model for other sports halls of fame, the collection is now part of the Amateur Athletic Foundation Headquarters on Adams Boulevard in Los Angeles. (Older photo courtesy of Amateur Athletic Foundation; recent photo taken by author.)

**JOHN ANSON FORD AND ESTHER WILLIAMS, 1952.** Born in Los Angeles, Esther Williams was on the 1940 Olympic swim team headed for Tokyo when World War II intervened, canceling the games, along with her hopes for the gold and international fame. Here is the same place she stood 50 years ago, carrying the torch to help commemorate so many other notable athletes. (Recent photo taken by author.)

**IN PREPARATION OF THE TORCH ARRIVAL, JANUARY 15, 2002.** En route to Salt Lake City, the torch visited the Coliseum, touching the building once more with a bit of Olympic history. (Photo taken by author.)

**AUTHOR AND SON, 2002.** We've tried to do this great place justice. Of course, it is impossible to include everything and I've tried to be as accurate as possible. In the meantime, I encourage you to visit this venerable stadium. Once here, I think you'll find it to be a special place. (Photo taken by Sally Struthers.)

128

CPSIA information can be obtained
at www.ICGtesting.com
Printed in the USA
BVOW07*1646050318
509717BV00013B/1390/P

9 781531 614140